CULTURE
in Indonesia

Melanie Guile

Heinemann
LIBRARY

First published 2002 by Heinemann Library
a division of Reed Education Australia,
18–22 Salmon Street, Port Melbourne Victoria 3207 Australia
(a division of Reed International Books Australia Pty Ltd, ABN 70 001 002 357).
Email info@hi.com.au
Website http://www.hi.com.au

℞ A Reed Elsevier company

06 05 04 03
10 9 8 7 6 5 4 3 2

Series cover and text design by Stella Vassiliou
Paged by Stella Vassiliou
Edited by Sarah Russell and Carmel Heron
Production by Michelle Sweeney
Pre-press by Digital Imaging Group (DIG), Melbourne
Printed in Hong Kong by Wing King Tong

National Library of Australia
Cataloguing-in-Publication data:

Guile, Melanie.
    Indonesia.

    Bibliography.
    Includes index.
    ISBN 1 74070 061 9.

    1. Indonesia – Civilization – Juvenile literature.
    2. Indonesia – Social life and customs – Juvenile literature.
    I. Title. (Series: Guile, Melanie, 1949– Culture in –).

959.8

Cover photograph of a *gamelan* orchestra in Bali supplied by Australian Picture Library.

Other photographs supplied by: Australian Picture Library: pp. 13, 15, 16, 17, 19, 20, 25;
Bill Bachman: p. 9; Coo-ee Picture Library: pp. 7, 11, 12, 27; Harald Melcher: p. 21;
Lochman Transparencies: pp. 23, 24; Photodisc: p. 29.

CONTENTS

Words that appear in
bold, **like this**, are explained
in the glossary on page 30.

CULTURE in Indonesia

 Pieces in the puzzle

The islands of the Indonesian **archipelago** are scattered like a giant jigsaw puzzle across the Equator, between South-East Asia and Australia. On a map, Indonesia is one nation, with a central, elected government, a capital city, one official, national language and an army of five million. But if you look closely at the pieces of the puzzle, a different picture emerges. With about 6000 inhabited islands, 365 languages and countless **ethnic groups**, Indonesia is made up of hundreds of distinct peoples with their own homelands, customs, traditions and cultures.

Women in Indonesia

Generally, Indonesian women are treated more equally than women in some other Muslim countries. Many do not wear veils, have at least a primary education and take jobs outside the home. Indonesia's president is a woman – Megawati Soekarnoputri.

 What is culture?

Culture is a people's way of living. It is the way people identify themselves as a group, separate and different from any other. Culture includes a group's language, social customs and habits, as well as its traditions of art, dance, music, writing and religion.

So what is Indonesian culture? From the Rambo-style Dayak gangs of Kalimantan to the strict **Muslim** *ulama* (religious teachers) of Aceh, ethnic groups do not see themselves as Indonesian at all. They call themselves Acehnese or Dayak, Papuan, Torajan or Javanese. To learn about the culture of Indonesia, we must explore the cultures of some of these **diverse** ethnic groups. Together they make up the full picture.

Rich cultural mix

Indonesia's rich cultural mix is a result of its place on the world's great trading routes. Indonesia was called the Spice Islands, and Indonesian spices were valuable **commodities** that attracted foreign traders and merchants. Indian merchants first brought the Hindu religion and writing to the people of the Indonesian archipelago. Later, Arab traders brought the religion and culture of **Islam**. Even today, half of the world's shipping passes through Indonesian waters.

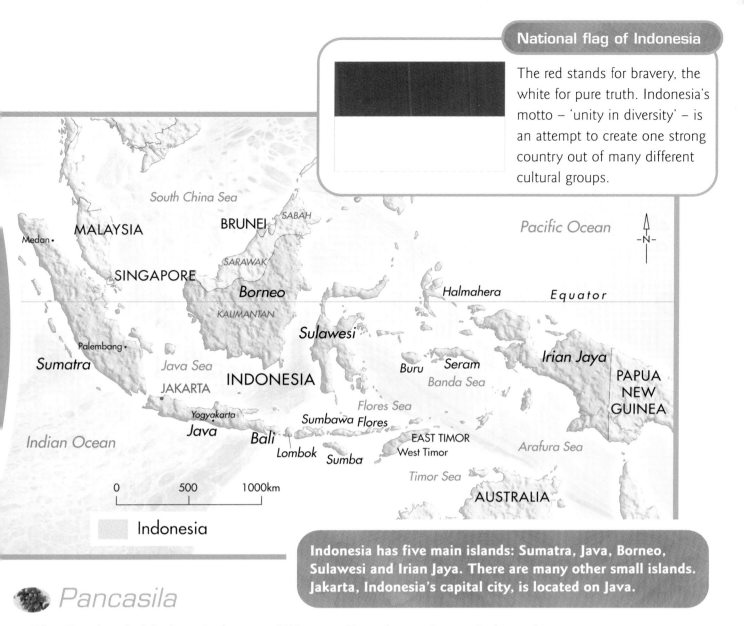

The red stands for bravery, the white for pure truth. Indonesia's motto – 'unity in diversity' – is an attempt to create one strong country out of many different cultural groups.

0   500   1000km

Indonesia

Indonesia has five main islands: Sumatra, Java, Borneo, Sulawesi and Irian Jaya. There are many other small islands. Jakarta, Indonesia's capital city, is located on Java.

Pancasila

The Dutch ruled Indonesia for over 350 years. Since becoming an independent nation in 1949, Indonesia has struggled to hold the pieces of the jigsaw together. Its first president, Soekarno, formed the idea of *Pancasila* – the five principles of faith in one god, humanity, **nationalism**, 'guided' **democracy** and social justice – which bind all Indonesian people together.

Although 87 per cent of Indonesia's 210 million people are Muslim, under *Pancasila* all main religions (Hinduism, Christianity and Buddhism) are permitted. Traditional tribal laws were replaced by national courts run from the capital city of Jakarta. Every child was offered primary education – as long as it was in the national language, Bahasa Indonesia. These measures made for strong government, but they tended to undermine local cultures.

Now the ties that bound Indonesia together as a nation are loosening. All over the archipelago, ethnic groups are demanding independence and the freedom to live according to their own laws, customs and principles.

5

CULTURE IN JAVA

The people of Java

Java is the smallest of Indonesia's five main islands, but it has dominated the culture of the whole archipelago since independence in 1949. Over half of Indonesia's 210 million people live on Java. The capital city and seat of government, Jakarta, lies on the island's north-western tip.

Three languages are spoken on Java – Javanese, Sundanese and Madurese. Most people also use Bahasa Indonesia as a second language. Many traditions that most Australians think of as Indonesian, such as shadow puppets and the *gamelan* orchestra, are in fact elements of Javanese culture.

Borneo

Sumatra

JAKARTA

Java

Bali Lombok

- Sundanese
- Madurese
- Javanese

-N-

This map of Java shows where the main cultural groups live.

Main ethnic groups

Two main ethnic groups inhabit the island: the Javanese (45 per cent of the Indonesian population) and the Sundanese (14 per cent) in West Java. The strictly Islamic Madurese come from the offshore island of Madura, but many now live on Java's north-east coast. Chinese people have lived in Java for hundreds of years, but they still suffer **discrimination**. Many ethnic Chinese have taken Indonesian names and tried to blend into the local culture.

Modern Java

Modern Java is a mix of many different races, cultures and beliefs. Each new cultural wave has melted into older customs, and the Javanese are very good at balancing contradictory elements. For example, some Islamic mosques have Hindu architectural features; at ritual feasts called *slametan* the old harvest gods are celebrated, but prayers are also offered to the Muslim god, Allah; and Java's syncretist sect of Islam includes **pagan** ancestor worship.

The Javanese led the push for democracy and reform in Indonesia, which held its first free elections in 1999. Generally, the Javanese see themselves as more advanced and sophisticated than other cultural groups in Indonesia.

Performing arts

Java has a rich heritage of theatre, dance and music, and there is also a lively modern performing arts scene.

Puppets

The famous shadow puppets – the *wayang kulit* – act out ancient Hindu **epics**, the *Ramayana* and *Mahabharata*. These are tales of beautiful princesses, powerful gods and mischievous monkeys. The puppets are intricately carved from flattened buffalo leather, and their arms are moved by long sticks. As their shadows flit across the lit screen, the puppeteer narrates the story to the accompaniment of the *gamelan* orchestra.

In West Java, the puppets of the *wayang golek* are three-dimensional painted wood, and their heads and arms are moved by sticks. In a version called the *wayang wong*, masked actors and dancers perform the traditional stories on stage.

'Losing face'

Self-control is important in Javanese society. Staying cool, calm and polite is essential if you want to gain respect. Aggressive or loud behaviour is frowned upon – especially for women. It is very important to avoid 'losing face' (being publicly made a fool of), so people seldom speak their mind or disagree openly. This can cause problems with more outspoken western tourists.

Modern theatre

Modern western-style theatre is popular in Jakarta and Yogyakarta. Plays often deal with political and social issues, usually via comedy or **satire**. This is one of the few ways Indonesians can express **political opposition**, although plays are often banned by the government.

Traditional and modern music

Gongs and drums form the chiming sounds of the traditional *gamelan* orchestra. Up to 80 musicians use a variety of metal percussion instruments, nowadays usually joined by xylophones, bamboo flutes and stringed instruments. *Gamelan* orchestras traditionally accompany the richly costumed Javanese dancers. The formal, slow, rigidly controlled movements of this dance take many years to learn. Like many aspects of Javanese culture, restraint and self-control are valued above spontaneity and self-expression.

Pop culture

From every radio, shop and *bemo* (public minibus) can be heard the hard beat of *dangdut* – Java's own rock dance music. It is influenced by American rock sounds, with echoes of traditional Malay music, Indian film scores and Arab pop. Java's king of *dangdut* is Rhoma Irama, whose songs combine religious, moral and social themes. His 1980 film musical *Struggle and Prayer* is probably the first-ever Islamic rock film.

West Java is the home of the modern dance craze *Jaipongan*. When western music and dancing were banned in the 1970s, a man called Gugum invented this social dance music. It is based on traditional Javanese dance with a bit of *silat* (a local form of kung fu) and lots of vigorous free movement. The music involves a female vocalist plus wild drumming from a backing group. So successful was the new dance with teenagers that the West Java government banned *Jaipongan* as well! Now it is legal, and danced all over Indonesia.

Songbird

Feared army chief General Wiranto is best known for his suppression of the East Timorese in their fight for independence. But it seems he has a softer side. He once startled a party of American **diplomats** by bursting into song with a version of the 1970s hit song, 'Feelings'. He was sacked from the army in 1999, and went on to record his first album entitled *For You My Indonesia*. The album consists of his ten favourite Indonesian soft-pop hits.

Batik fabric dyeing is a traditional Javanese craft.

Batik cloth

Batik is made by intricate designs being 'painted' (*batik tulis*) or stamped (*batik cap*) with melted wax on cloth, and the cloth is then dyed. When the wax is washed off, the cloth is re-dyed in different colours.

Javanese food

Many Javanese are Muslim and do not eat pork or drink alcohol. Their basic diet consists of steamed rice served with small side dishes of fish, beef and vegetables, with chilli and spicy sauces to add flavour. Dishes from every corner of the world are available in the restaurants and stalls of big Javanese cities, such as Jakarta and Yogyakarta. Chinese food first came to Java hundreds of years ago. Now it is a popular alternative to the more spicy local fare. Most of the best known Indonesian dishes such as *gado-gado* (vegetables in spicy peanut sauce) and *sate* (sticks of barbequed meat) came originally from Java.
During the holy month of Ramadan, **devout** Muslims do not eat, drink or smoke cigarettes from dawn to sunset.

CULTURE IN BALI

The people of Bali

Only a few kilometres of ocean separate the island of Bali from neighbouring Java, but the two cultures are worlds apart. The Balinese are easygoing, artistic people who practise a blend of Hinduism, Buddhism and ancient spirit worship. The population of around 3.5 million is almost all ethnic Balinese. Unlike other ethnic groups in Indonesia the Balinese remain largely in charge of their own land.

Their fertile and beautiful island has offered wonderful holidays for tourists who flooded to Bali from around the world, bringing great prosperity. European-style hotels, shops and entertainments choke areas such as Kuta Beach, and the Balinese see tourism as a modern extension of their strong tradition of welcoming and entertaining visitors. However, following a terrorist bomb in October 2002, the number of travellers to the island reduced to a trickle, with devastating consequences for the many Balinese involved in the tourist industry.

Java

Bali

Lombok

Sumba

Indian Ocean

Balinese

–N–

The island of Bali

Village life

For the Balinese, life centres around the family and the village. Everyone owes a duty to the community, and is expected to abide by traditional rules and customs. Each family lives in a walled compound that holds several *bale* (traditional thatched houses without walls). Every village has a large *bale banjar* for meetings and village activities.

Many Balinese are farmers and grow rice in terraced fields called paddies. These are flooded at planting time using a complex **irrigation** system. Village groups called *subak* make sure all the paddies fields get a fair share of the water. Balinese culture emphasises cooperation and community above competition and individuality.

Religion

The spirits are never far away on Bali, and little shrines and temples for them are found in rice paddies, on roadsides or under trees. Every village has its own temples – to the ancestors, to the community's guiding spirits, and to the dead. Villagers make offerings of food and flowers to them daily. Temples are also found in private houses and universities, and daily offerings are put in the temples and corners of shops – even in very modern shopping plazas.

Gunung Agung, an active volcano, is sacred to the Balinese and their most important temple, *Pura Besakih* (the Mother Temple), is built on its rumbling slopes. The Balinese pray to the great god Sanghyang Widi at the building of a new house, and also worship the Hindu gods. In Bali, religion is more celebration than duty, and hundreds of festivals, feasts and dances punctuate the year. However, religion is very strictly observed. For example, during the quiet 'Nyepi Day', tourists are asked not to leave their hotels, and shops and other businesses are closed.

Tough tactics

The Balinese protect their thriving and valuable tourist industry, with force if need be. After a series of attacks on tourists by gangs, traders organised groups of locals to patrol the streets. Anyone found **loitering** was moved on.

11

Festivals

At *Galungan* festival, the gods come to Earth to enjoy ten days of feasts, dancing and singing. Villagers decorate very tall, curved bamboo poles and hang them with thanksgiving offerings of fruit, rice and beautifully made palm-leaf decorations. The Barong, a friendly god with huge fangs, bulbous eyes and a long mane, drives evil spirits from the houses. Barong and Rangda the evil witch are traditional enemies, and many stories and dances act out battles between them.

Not all Balinese festivals are traditional. At Sanur Beach, where magnificent surf brings many international visitors, the first Surfing Attraction Festival was held in 2001. Bali Fashion Week (held in May) showcases the work of local fashion designers and fabric makers. Styles are graceful and wearable, and make use of modern versions of rich Balinese fabrics like *ikats, batiks* and silk sarongs. The town of Ubud is a vibrant centre of modern art, with many local painters and sculptors.

Performing arts

In Bali, dance, music and song are a gift to the gods. Prayers and offerings are made before a dance to ask for *taksu* (inspiration) and dances tell religious stories where good gods battle evil and always win. These tales include giants, witches, graceful princesses and brave heroes, and they often involve changing moods of slapstick humour, high drama and romance. The *Kecak* dance takes its name from the 'cak-cak-cak' chant of a choir who dance and sing the story of the Hindu Prince Rama and Sita, his wife, in a tale of kidnap, war and rescue, with the help of the magical monkey Hanuman.

Women carry offerings of fruit, rice and flowers to temples.

The famous *Legong* is a slow, graceful court dance in which two richly costumed young women move together in a mix of poses, arm and foot movements. Traditional dances change all the time as new versions are developed.

Funerals

In Bali, when a person dies, a great tower is made to carry the body. It is built of bamboo, and represents heaven at the top, the Earth at the base and the dead person lying in between at the start of its journey to the gods. The whole tower is richly decorated with brilliant flowers, fabric, paper and other trinkets. The funeral procession runs, twists and circles around to the tune of the *gamelan* orchestra to confuse the ghost so it will not come back to haunt the living. Finally, the tower with the body is burnt and the ashes scattered in the river or the sea.

An elaborately decorated funeral tower. Later it is burned with the body.

Caste system

Hindu Balinese have a caste, or class, system. Brahmans, the priests, are at the top and almost everyone else belongs to the Sudra caste. Balinese language can be used at three different levels of respect. Priests in Bali use a special language (*Ida*) at religious ceremonies, but distinctions like this are dying out.

CULTURE
in Sumatra

The people of Sumatra

Hundreds of years ago, Sumatra was the centre of a great trading empire, controlling the sea lanes between India and China. Today, Sumatra's 45 million people are still proudly independent. Many different cultural groups live in this resource-rich island. The main ones are the Muslim Acehnese on the northern tip, the Christian Bataks, and the restless Minangkabau in the west. With such different ethnic groups, Sumatra has always been a place of conflict. Since independence in 1949, the Indonesian army has kept control, but at great cost to human rights. Now ethnic groups are demanding freedom to rule themselves and preserve their unique cultures.

The Acehnese

Strictly Muslim, and with a distinct culture and language, the Acehnese have never accepted government from Java. 'To be Acehnese is to be Muslim,' they say, and they regard themselves as more devout and courageous than other Indonesians. They are proud that they were never conquered during 500 years of Dutch rule. The Acehnese regard *Pancasila* as another attempt to destroy their unique culture. Although the Indonesian Government has promised the Acehnese **self-rule** it has never kept its word. Since 1976, the Free Aceh Movement (*Aceh Merdeka*) has waged a **guerrilla** war against the Indonesian army.

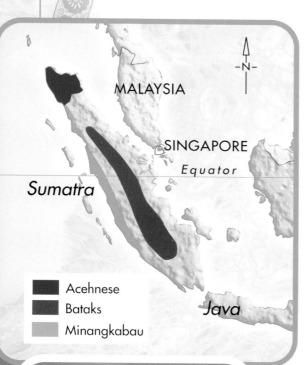

Map of Sumatra showing areas where Muslim Acehnese live (on the northern tip), where Bataks live, and where the Minangkabau live (in the west).

The rebel flag of Aceh

Armed rebels want an independent state in Aceh based on a **moderate** form of Islamic law. Thousands of rebels have been killed fighting the Indonesian army, and many citizens are refugees from the violence.

An Acehnese woman selling produce at a market in Sumatra

Acehnese culture

Women have more power in Aceh. They make decisions about the home and children, and property is passed down through the mother. After marriage, the husband joins the wife in her village. Women wear veils and Islamic law is very strict in limiting women's behaviour outside the home. Islam controls every aspect of the people's lives. Children learn to read the Koran (the holy book) at the of age of seven, and perform religious duties. Every Friday, mosques in Aceh are packed with believers for prayers and sermons called *khotbah*, often used for political speeches.

The Acehnese have around 50 types of traditional dances. The *saman,* or 'thousand hands', was originally a folk dance of the Alas tribal group, but now it is performed to celebrate **Mohammed's** birthday. Dancers kneel in a row and move their arms faster and faster, clapping hands and slapping their chests, accompanied by music and prayers. In the *daboih* dance, young men pretend to stab themselves with knives, blades and even chainsaws, all to the beat of a tambourine (*rapa-ii*). Strings, wind instruments and percussion similar to the Javanese *gamelan* orchestra are common in Acehnese music, but may be joined by the haunting sound of the *arbab*, a three-stringed zither made of jackfruit wood, or the bamboo flute (*seurunee kalee*).

The Bataks

The Bataks are very different from their nearest northern neighbours, the Acehnese. Around six million Bataks live inland in mountain valleys, where they build their distinctive scoop-roofed houses. These houses are made of wood lashed together without nails, and built on stilts with no windows and one door. The huge peaked gables are richly carved and decorated. Traditionally, a moat and barrier also surrounded each village. The Batak are excellent farmers, and export vegetables all over Indonesia.

Batak beliefs

Most Bataks now speak and write Bahasa Indonesia, but have their own ancient written language. It was used to record myths and prayers in religious rituals, and the writing was carved on bamboo or bone. Although converted to Christianity by **missionaries**, the Bataks still respect the spirits and ghosts that watch over their world. The banyan tree is sacred, and Batak myths say all living things came from it through the work of the creator god, Ompung. Each Batak respects his *tondi* (his or her own spirit-soul) and makes sacrifices to it, and at harvest time ceremonies thank the spirits.

The Bataks build richly carved and decorated houses.

Cannibals

Before the 1800s, when missionaries arrived, the Batak believed that eating the flesh of enemies gave them power and courage. Heads were cooked over open fires, and slices of flesh were eaten as part of a ritual feast. Villagers who broke traditional laws (*adat*) were also eaten.

Love of dance

Like the Acehnese, the Minangkabau love to dance. Most famous of their dances is the *Tari Lilin*, the candle dance. Performed by women in brilliant costumes, the dance involves balancing lighted candles in bowls in the hands while twisting and turning in quick, graceful movements. The women's headscarves are shaped to resemble buffalo horns, traditionally sacred to the Minangkabau.

In the *Tari Piring*, men dance on heaps of broken china. At important celebrations, like weddings and harvests, the *Randai* is performed. Twenty players act out and dance traditional myths and legends from Minangkabau literature. At the Muslim festival of *Tabut*, villagers make mythical figures called *bouraq* (winged horses with women's heads) and parade with them through the streets. The figures are then thrown into the sea and villagers compete to retrieve them.

The Minangkabau

The Minangkabau of West Sumatra are Muslim. They have a reputation for being adaptable, hard-working, confident and articulate. The Minangkabau have migrated all over the archipelago and been successful in business.

Minangkabau life is run by the women who control household, property, family and village matters. Rural families live in large group huts with huge scooped roofs, similar to Batak houses. The Minangkabau have thrived under *Pancasila* because they can embrace other cultures and new ideas while maintaining their traditional customs (*adat*).

Ethnic success

The Minangkabau are Indonesia's fourth largest ethnic group and one of its most prosperous. Shrewd traders and politicians, they have the highest literacy rate in the country. The first modern Indonesian poet, Muhammed Yamin, was Minang. His most famous poem is 'Tanah Air' ('My Fatherland'), written in 1920.

CULTURE
in Irian Jaya

The people of Irian Jaya

In the remote rainforests of Irian Jaya (the Indonesian name for West Papua), **indigenous** people have lived undisturbed for 40 000 years. Papuans are related to Australian Aboriginal people who, it is thought, came to Australia from Papua via land bridges that were later cut off by sea. About 250 different tribal groups live in the highlands of Irian Jaya and along the southern coast, separated from each other by impassable peaks and crocodile-infested **marshes**. Each group has its own language, customs, beliefs and way of living, and they all share a deep spiritual bond with the land.

Cultures under threat

The ancient cultures of Irian Jaya are under threat. Government-sponsored migrants from Java and Bali outnumber local Irian Jayans in some areas, causing tension and unrest among traditional owners. Loggers from Sulawesi strip the rainforest and miners pollute the rivers that local people depend on. Huge foreign-owned **palm oil** and coffee plantations squeeze out Papuan **subsistence farmers**, and church missionaries urge them to give up their traditional religions.

The principles of *Pancasila* (one god, humanity, nationalism, democracy and social justice) are meaningless in Irian Jaya, where **corruption** is rife and justice is brutal in the hands of the Indonesian army. But the people of Irian Jaya are now demanding control of their homeland, and the different cultural groups are uniting to fight for independence from Indonesia.

A map of Irian Jaya showing where the Dani live (Baliem Valley), where the Asmat live (south coast), and where the Korowai live

Flag of West Papua

The 'Morning Star' is the flag of West Papua and the symbol of the Free Papua Movement. It is illegal to raise this flag anywhere in Indonesia.

The Dani of the Baliem Valley

The rich culture of the Dani people of the Baliem Valley was unknown to outsiders until some western bushwalkers came upon them by accident in 1938. Most Dani are farmers, raising pigs and growing vegetables. About three to six families live in a cluster of huts surrounded by a fence of sharpened stakes. Within this compound are the men's and women's huts, pig pens and vegetable plots. The round thatched huts (*honay*) are made of split logs, with double walls for **insulation** and a woven palm-leaf floor. A ladder leads to a loft for sleeping under the thatched roof. Dani men and women sleep in separate huts.

Ancient customs and beliefs

When a family member died, Dani warriors raided neighbouring clans to collect heads so that the natural balance of deaths would be restored. Eating the flesh of relatives was seen as a tribute to the dead person. Female relatives had a finger joint chopped off as a sign of mourning, and old women can still be seen with missing fingers.

Today most Dani are Christian, but they respect the ancestors in funeral and other rituals. Mourners come from many villages, with pig fat and ashes smeared over their bodies. They bring gifts of food and wail by the corpse until it is set alight. Sometimes these ceremonies end in violence as old tribal grudges resurface.

Tourist takeover

Tourism is growing in the Baliem Valley, but the Dani are not reaping the benefits. Javanese businessmen control the tourist industry and will not employ the locals. Dani people are farmers and inexperienced in business, so profits go to outsiders. Now Dani groups are demanding a fair share of tourist wealth.

The Asmat

Long feared as ferocious headhunters and cannibals, the Asmat have inhabited the south coast of Irian Jaya for thousands of years. About 65 000 Asmat live in **tidal swamps** where, in spite of harsh conditions, they create brilliant works of art in the form of carved wooden shields, spirit figures, masks, drums and weapons. These works represent spirits and ghosts that the Asmat believe live in every part of their environment – the rivers, trees, animals and the sky.

Ancient beliefs

The Asmat regard death as a normal return to *safan*, the spirit world surrounding them. Traditionally, every violent death had to be 'paid for' in enemy heads, because the dead people's spirits could not rest otherwise. In southern Asmat, skulls of family members were used as pillows and worn around the neck for good luck.

Made from mangrove roots, Asmat warriors' shields are painted and carved with head-hunting symbols to terrify enemies. Shield owners believed the spirit within their shields made them **invincible**.

Today the Asmat respect the spirits through their art and many rituals. During the mask feast, ancestors visit the living and reassure them of their help and guidance. Magic spells and potions ward off evil spirits and ghosts. The Asmat see themselves as connected spiritually to the forest – their feet are roots, their bodies are trunks, their arms branches, and their heads the fruit. Their name means 'real people' in contrast to the dead, the spirits and outsiders.

Art in demand

Asmat works of art are becoming so popular with tourists and collectors that the quality of the art work is declining, as roughly made works are sold for quick cash. Nevertheless, Asmat masks are displayed in fine art galleries around the world.

The Korowai

Hemmed in by huge mountains and large rivers, the Korowai have lived locked away from the world for thousands of years. Tribal warfare and a harsh environment dominate their daily lives. Even today, payback (revenge) killings are a normal part of life, and kidnapping women and pigs is common among enemy tribes. All the energy of the Korowai is given to survival and to building their extraordinary tree houses. About 2500 Korowai occupy swampy land that is no good for farming.

They hunt, fish and gather **sago** from the bark of palm trees. Dugout canoes provide transport, and all work is done without metals. Stone axes and bone knives are used to strip the bark from sago palms, and wooden bows and arrows help the men to catch birds, snakes, crocodiles and frogs for meat.

Korowai houses

The most spectacular aspect of the culture of the Korowai is their houses. They live in thatched grass huts built on platforms high up in trees. The huts are reached by climbing notched branches or twig ladders. Normally built from 6 to 25 metres up for protection from enemy raids, these houses take up to eight people in separate men's and women's huts.

Korowai tree houses can be built up to 50 metres above the forest floor during tribal wars.

Threatened way of life

The Korowai's extraordinary culture may be disappearing. The Indonesian government in Java has ordered changes to their ancient way of life. Korowai are now leaving their family tree houses and living in huts with other clans. Disease, tribal warfare and unrest have resulted, and the numbers of Korowai are falling.

CULTURE OF THE
Dayaks of Kalimantan

The Dayak people

Remote and inaccessible, the jungles of Kalimantan are home to the Dayak tribes. It is thought that they migrated to the island of Borneo thousands of years ago in waves from southern China, and their light skin and almond eyes support this theory. When Malay and Arab traders invaded the coast, these sea-going people fled in their long boats up the rivers into the rainforests, where they still live.

Dayaks

A map of Borneo showing where the Dayaks live

Around two million Dayak people live in Borneo, half of these in the Indonesian part called Kalimantan. There are six main tribal groups. The most famous are the Ibans (Sea Dayaks), once known as pirates and ruthless head-hunters. The Punans roam the jungle as hunter-gatherer nomads, and build only temporary houses. Most Dayak groups live in riverside villages where they farm rice, pigs and chickens. They also hunt and fish. Traditionally war-like, the Dayaks have a strong sense of ownership of their land and have always resisted any attempts by Borneo traders, immigrants or missionaries to change their ancient customs and beliefs.

'Ethnic cleansing'

Since the 1960s, the Indonesian Government has sent settlers from Java and Madura to Kalimantan to work on plantations and in mines. The Dayaks resent these settlers because they earn money from Dayak resources and destroy the rainforest through logging and pollution. In February 2001, Dayak raiders killed and beheaded hundreds of Madurese. Thousands of settlers fled in terror from Kalimantan, and any who try to return are swiftly killed by the Dayaks.

A Dayak communal house, called a *lamin*. Traditionally, up to 50 families would live in these long houses.

Village life

Cooperation and family kinship are important to the Dayaks. Traditionally, up to 50 families live in huge long houses called *lamin*. These houses are raised on stilts for coolness and shelter for the animals, and at night rope ladders are pulled up for safety. Many Dayak long houses have richly carved panels, with dragons, snakes, birds and spirit figures. Inside, palm-leaf screens separate the families, and everyone gathers under the long veranda, where washing is hung and children play. The family elder lives in the middle room. This way of living leaves no room for privacy or individual needs, but provides shared responsibility and great security for members of the group.

Many villagers still live in long houses, but other Dayaks have been forced off their traditional lands by logging and mining companies into crowded, poverty-stricken towns where Islam and western-style culture threaten their way of life.

Headhunting

Warfare between Dayak groups has been a way of life for centuries. Dayak men raided neighbouring clans and brought home human heads as prizes. Young warriors called up Bali Akang, the spirit of courage, and set out head-hunting to earn their manhood. Success was rewarded with special body tattoos and general rejoicing. Heads taken had the brains sucked out and were smoked over fires to preserve them. It was believed that the heads gave spiritual energy to the clan, protected them from harm and encouraged good harvests. Headhunting is banned in Kalimantan, but even today the bodies of murder victims are often found headless.

Festivals

At rice harvest in June, a 'water-dripping' ceremony (called a *siram*) mimics the rain, and encourages the river spirits to float away. *Katang* is a yearly ceremony to chase away evil spirits from the village. Rotten eggs and other smelly things are tied to decorated *belawang* poles outside the village, and all paths in and out are blocked for three days so the spirits cannot return. Animals slaughtered for the gods at festivals give magic power. But Dayaks are generally not cruel to their animals; in fact, they ask the pig's forgiveness before they kill it!

The modern Dayak religion is a blend of Christian and ancient spiritual beliefs. This Dayak woman is dancing to honour a deceased relative.

Crafts and customs

The Dayak are artistic. They weave colourful *ikat* cloth, make iron and steel weapons for hunting and produce spectacular masks. Even simple items are decorated to represent the sacred world that rules Dayak life. Palm-leaf weaving, called rattan, is used for baskets, sleeping mats, screens, houses and even baby-carriers. These backpacks for infants are patterned with seeds, dogs' teeth, shells and glass beads as charms to ward off evil. Feathers of the sacred hornbill bird protect the baby, and mask-like designs represent spirit faces, although today the power of such charms is fading with modern influences.

Sick relatives are often put in the hands of the village *wadian,* or traditional healer. Usually an old woman, the *wadian* performs dances over the sick person, identifies the cause of the trouble and communicates with the spirits in a trance to cure the patient. If the person dies, unique funeral rites are held to help the dead spirit reach the next world. Traditionally, a richly carved and decorated ship of death was made and the body placed in it and launched down river. Nowadays, coffins in the shape of ships are buried in Christian graveyards.

Pierced and stretched ear lobes were a sign of beauty for traditional Dayak women. Larger and heavier metal rods or rings were gradually placed in the pierced ears so they stretched – often reaching halfway down the chest.

Dayak religion

All Dayak groups recognise Belare, the thunder ghost. When he opens his mouth, thunder roars; when he winks, lightning flashes. Modern Dayak religion is a blend of Christian and ancient spiritual beliefs. Only the Ibans (Sea Dayaks) have adopted Islam.

CULTURE OF THE
Toraja of Sulawesi

On the south-western arm of the island of Sulawesi is Tanatoraja, the land of the Toraja people. Their name means 'mountain people', and legends tell how their ancestors sailed up the great Sa'dan River to settle in the jungle highlands. They are farming people who grow rice, coffee and vegetables, and raise pigs, chickens and dogs for food. Water buffalo are sacred and a form of wealth to the Toraja people, so they are killed only for special festivals. About 500 000 Toraja now live in Sulawesi, but many more have left to find work in more prosperous parts of Indonesia.

Like many tribal groups in Indonesia today, the Toraja combine ancient beliefs and myths with more recent cultural influences. Although strongly Christian, they maintain ancient customs honouring the spirits and ancestors, most famously in their lavish funeral ceremonies.

Toraja

'Hot toddy'

It is said that the Toraja resisted the Islamic religion because it outlawed palm wine (*tuak*) and pork, which are their favourite treats. Christian missionaries, on the other hand, tolerated the wine (which they called toddy), made from the sweet sap of the sugar palm.

A map of Sulawesi showing where the Toraja live

The peaked roofs of traditional Torajan houses. These houses now play an important part in religious and community life.

Village houses

Torajan traditional houses called *tongkonan* have huge scooped roofs with high peaks. They are made of bamboo and wood fitted together, and no nails are used. Intricate painted carvings decorate the outside walls and gables, and a carved and painted buffalo head over the entrance brings good luck. Extra horns decorate the front pole to show how wealthy the family is. Animals are sacrificed before a *tongkonan* is built to bring luck and pay tribute to the ancestors. Once, human heads were a vital part of this ceremony, and young warriors were sent to slice them from enemy tribespeople. Only rich and powerful families were allowed to build *tongkonan*. In fact, status is very important in Torajan society, which has upper and lower class members, and once had slaves too. Many traditional houses are now kept only for ceremonies, but they are still a vital part of religious and community life.

Food

For Torajans rice is the main food, usually cooked simply, with pork or chicken and vegetables from the village plots. At festival time or for visitors, more elaborate dishes are made. *Pa'piong* consists of green leafy vegetables with chicken and coconut milk cooked over a fire in bamboo tubes. Pork is sometimes used too. Although far from the sea, the Toraja enjoy fish, which is brought in by road from the coast, and eels that are caught in the flooded paddy fields. Coffee is grown in Tanatoraja, and exported all over the world. The local people drink it strong and sweet.

Soul rites

The Toraja believe each person has a sacred soul that must be cared for. When a family member is ill, the Toraja believe the soul has wandered from the person's body. Priests called *to minaa* call it back with magical chants.

To guide dead souls into the next world and keep them there, elaborate funeral ceremonies called *tomate* are held. These last up to seven days and attract thousands of guests. The body is preserved, offered food, then carried to a burial platform, where men sing of the dead person's life and perform a long ritual dance. Precious buffalo, pigs and chickens are killed to provide for the dead person's journey. Buffalo blood is caught in bamboo poles for drinking, and the meat is offered to guests. Huge outdoor kitchens are set up to feed the guests, who must bring presents of buffalo, pigs and cigarettes. So expensive are these funerals that families can take years to save up for one. The Indonesian Government discourages them by levying a tax on each buffalo killed.

Tree burials

The dead ride to heaven (*puya*) on the backs of pigs or buffalo killed for the funeral. Babies were considered to be too little to ride, so they were traditionally buried in hollows of trees. The tree's sap provided the dead child with mother's milk, and the tree spirit held it safe until it was old enough to ride into heaven.

Some less wealthy Torajan families bury their dead in chambers in cliff faces.

Burying the dead

Wealthy Torajan families are buried in rock caves carved from cliffs. Favourite possessions such as buffalo, pigs or gold are buried with the body, so wooden doors protect each cave from grave robbers. Dummies called *tau tau* are carved and dressed to look like the dead person, then arranged on balconies on the cliff face to guard the graves and bring luck to the living. Less wealthy families bury their dead in grave houses, natural caves or coffins hanging from cliffs or trees. Many Torajans return from all over Indonesia for the 'funeral season' between July and September.

GLOSSARY

archipelago   a group of islands in a sea

commodity   a product that is bought and sold

corruption   dishonesty; criminal activities, such as taking bribes, by government officials or other powerful people

democracy   a form of government in which the citizens of a country vote to choose their leaders

devout   very religious

diplomat   a representative of a foreign government

discrimination   unfair or unequal treatment based on a difference of race, sex or religion

diverse   various kinds or forms

epics long poems telling stories about heroes

ethnic groups   groups of people from different countries and cultures

guerrilla   someone who belongs to a secret, undercover group that wages war on an enemy; a guerrilla war involves a group or groups of undercover fighters fighting a common enemy

indigenous   native to a country or region

insulation   material to reduce extremes of heat or cold (in buildings)

invincible   unable to be harmed or killed

irrigation   an artificial crop watering system

Islam   the Muslim religion, which is based on believing in one god and the teachings of the prophet Mohammed

loitering   lingering; hanging about

marshes   low-lying watery or boggy land

missionaries   people who do religious work, often in foreign countries

moderate   medium; not too little or too much

Mohammed   the Arab founder of Islam

Muslim   follower of the Islamic religion

nationalism   a strong commitment to your nation and the desire for it to be free and self-governing

pagan   not Christian, Jewish or Islamic; worshipping many gods

palm oil   oil made from palm trees

political opposition   disagreement with the government in power

sago   a starchy foodstuff found inside the trunks of palm trees and used to make puddings and other dishes

satire   a work that makes fun of people or their behaviour and beliefs

self-rule   rule by the people of their own state, not by outsiders

subsistence farmers   farmers who grow just enough food to feed their family or group

tidal swamps   boggy land that fills with seawater at high tide

FURTHER *information*

Books

Fisher, F. *Countries of the World* series – *Indonesia*. Times Editions, Singapore, 2000.

Mesenas, G. and F. Fisher. *Welcome to My Country* series – *Welcome to Indonesia*. Times Editions, Singapore, 2001.

Thompson, L. *Fighting for Survival* series – *The Dani of Irian Jaya*. Reed Library. Cardigan Street, Melbourne, 1997.

Townsend, S. and C. Young. *A World of Recipies – Indonesia*. Heinemann Library, Oxford, 2003.

Websites

For further information about Indonesian arts and culture, festivals, food and recipes:

www.asianinfo.org/asianinfo/indonesia/about_indonesia.htm

www.gergo.com/webconnections/indonesia

INDEX

T

WITHDRAWN